Love Your Life, Shine Your Light

Inner Reflections to Build Your Best Life by Becoming Aware of What is Within

This book is dedicated to liberation
from limiting beliefs,
from the parts of ourselves we choose to protect with denial,
from our resistance to change,
from the thoughts we feed that allow us to remain small,
from dead end jobs, relationships, and lifestyles,
from repressed emotions and unmanaged minds,
from self-defense mechanisms that exist to control others' perceptions of us,
from caring about how it looks instead of how it truly feels,
from being numb,
from living on autopilot,
from discontentment, unfulfillment, and from settling.

Here's to a liberated mind, a renewed spirit, a restored heart, and a transformed life!

Never forget: What's on the inside matters!

Contents

1. Decide / 6
2. Creating Vision as a Student of Yourself / 11
3. Next Level Thoughts That Create Next Level Results / 16
4. Beliefs That Create or Eliminate the Possibilities That Live in Your Future / 21
5. Trust Your Process / 26
6. You Are Meant for More / 30
7. Being in the Driver's Seat in Your Life / 34
8. Doing Whatever It Takes to Become Your Best / 39
9. The Power of Belief and Taking Action / 43
10. Building Credibility With Yourself / 48
11. Boundaries Start With You / 53
12. Getting Results With Consistency and Intentionality / 58
13. Invest in You / 63
14. Centered in Self-Care / 68
15. Ask for What You Need / 72
16. Envisioning and Creating Your Desired Life / 76
17. Start Living Your Dream / 81
18. Push Past Hard Things With Belief / 86
19. Allow Your Knowledge To Fuel Your Actions / 91
20. Permission to be Vulnerable / 95
21. The Prescription / 100
22. Growth / 105
23. Rejection is Not a Reflection of Me / 110
24. Choose What's in Your Best Interest / 114
25. Live Anyway / 118
26. Let it Go / 122
27. Walk in Truth / 126
28. What Are You Making it Mean / 130
29. Find Your People / 135
30. Honoring Others by First Honoring Yourself / 139
31. I Am Worthy / 144
32. Believe in Your Vision / 148
33. Appearance Isn't Everything / 153

Introduction

Many of us have created lives unconsciously based upon familial and societal expectations. We have been taught the essential ingredients to living a good life are: graduating from school, securing a "good" job, getting into a relationship, creating a family, buying a home, purchasing a dream car, etc. You fill in the blanks with your ingredients and you will find the path to the basics.

I made the decision to write this book because I value connection, community, communication, authenticity, and living in alignment with the desires of my soul.

I believe society's blueprint creates for us a basic lifestyle and we were created to live exceptionally! Here, I share reflections on my journey of learning to love my life so that I can better shine light on others in hopes that they can do the same.

Discovering the ingredients that create an exceptional life allows us to show up in an unapologetic and powerfully authentic way. A way where connection is built by the truth of our shared experience and experiences that reveal the purpose of our pain.

In a technological world where people have access to so much information and can easily share the highlights of their lives, I see so many who often share their success but shy away from the messes. I wonder, what is it that keeps us from sharing the messes that make those positive experiences that much sweeter? What would it look, feel and be like to operate in the fullness of our humanity and to fully love and value all aspects of our lives? What would it feel like to not be so self-conscious about sharing our lives through the lens of vulnerability? How would learning to love and shine light on every part of our lives, empower others to do the same? How could operating in this love allow us to better love others and inspire them to walk in their own light?

As I share nuggets from my own story, I invite you to journey with me. Join me as I push myself past my comfort zone and share vulnerable pieces of my story.

At the end of every passage there will be an opportunity for you to take time and journal your reflections on the passage. You are welcome to journal for as little or as long as you'd like.

It is my hope that as you turn the following pages, you will be inspired to think in new ways; that you muster up the courage to try something that feels scary. Allow yourself to reflect on the life lessons embedded in your story and become more aware of what's within you. May you feel less alone as you journey toward building a life you feel proud of.

Decide

Many of us live much of our lives going through the motions, checking off checklists of expectations: graduate high school, go to college and graduate, get the car you desire, live somewhere you like, get married, have kids and find a career you enjoy. All the while not allowing ourselves to fully experience our emotions during the process, never fully being present in those moments because we are looking to check off the next to do. Not even allowing ourselves to think about what we *really* want. Simply jumping through the hoops of life believing that when we check off all the tasks, *then* we can find joy and fulfillment.

What I know for certain is that as I began to work my way through my own checklist of life, I was doing all the "expected" things, all while feeling numb. I wasn't living. I was merely existing, to "do" the things that "created" a good life. Over time, I've learned that life is not about the destination but the journey. We are given all the information about how to survive, but aren't taught how to find meaning and fulfillment along the way.

I had to experience great discomfort to finally come to the realization that I wasn't living authentically according to who I am, but to whom others expected me to be. That's when I began to get clear about the kind of life I wanted, and began doing the work to create it.

There is so much more to life than simply checking off the to-do lists. There are opportunities and experiences waiting to be had.

Will you allow yourself the gift of living a fulfilled, authentic life or settle for doing what society expects of you? The choice is yours.

Letting go of superficial expectations has freed me to rediscover who I am and the kind of life I want to live.

Today, I encourage you to do the same. Think of something that is life-giving for you and go do it. That is the first step.

You get to decide how your days are spent. I gently nudge you to do something life-giving for yourself today.

REFLECTIONS:

After reading this passage, I realize:

Affirmation: ***I will live my life authentically according to who I am.***

Questions to process:

What more do I want in my life?

What aspects of my life do I want to enjoy more?

After answering the questions above, I now understand:

Moving forward, I will:

Creating Vision as a Student of Yourself

I believe it takes more than executing goals to live a fulfilling life. Self-awareness and understanding are essential. How do I know this? I'm living proof. From a very young age, I was told, "If you want something you work for it. Set goals and achieve them." And that's just what I did. Post-high school, I said "yes" to a series of goals (syllabi) for eight years straight. I received a Bachelor of Arts in psychology and religion at age twenty-one, a Master of Social Work at twenty-three and a Master of Divinity at age twenty-five. Each time I walked across the graduation stage, I could feel everyone else's excitement and positive energy.

But, why didn't I feel accomplished after I had received such a high level of achievement? Why did I feel numb? The answer didn't come to me until after I had my daughter three years later. It was the first time in my life I truly *felt* that I had worked and sacrificed for something I believed in. After months of reflection, I realized I had spent the first twenty-eight years of my life living by the values, standards and expectations of my family. I had never taken the time to realize my own.

Motherhood has taught me how important it is to establish an authentic foundation. Pre-motherhood, I was a student of everything and everyone, except myself. I kind of knew what I liked, valued, desired and expected, but I never processed *why*. I had never been challenged to ask myself deeper questions that generated greater self-understanding. I didn't even know what those questions were.

I now understand the power of knowing my value and temperament, unique strengths and limitations, blindspots and defense mechanisms, coping mechanisms, limited beliefs, standards and boundaries, and communication style. I've come to the conclusion that results tend to have more significance when you give the process all you have–with a clear understanding of why the result is so valuable to *you*. Taking the time to better understand my personality, wants, needs and outcomes has made it easier for me to reach my goals. This level of self-awareness has enabled me to better relate to others, know how to specifically articulate my needs and take the necessary action to create more of what I want in my life. In order to generate an authentic goal, you must first listen to what lies within.

REFLECTIONS:

After reading this passage, I realize:

Affirmation: **I give myself permission to look within with great compassion, non-judgment and curiosity. I am grateful for what I find because the truth provides building blocks that allow me to build a life of fulfillment.**

Questions to process:

What do I believe to be most important in my life?

Where do these beliefs come from and why are they important to me?

REFLECTIONS:

After answering the questions above, I now understand:

Moving forward I will:

Next Level Thoughts That Create Next Level Results

I've always desired to have access to the best things in life. I used to classify the best things as material things: degrees, a good job, nice cars, marriage and material wealth. Although those things are nice to have, I have learned that the best things in life circulate around mental, physical, emotional, spiritual, financial, and relational well-being.

To maintain a healthy and balanced life, you need vision, belief, intentionality, routine and healthy habits. I realized that in order to maintain my health, I had to let go of negative thinking and self-talk, toxic relationships, impulsivity and procrastination. The journey has not been easy. I had no idea just how harsh my inner critic was until I committed to a thirty day gratitude journaling experience with one of my best friends.

We wrote about the different aspects of our day that we were grateful for and processed with each other the following day. I left every conversation realizing how much I take for granted. I also realized how much I chose to look at everything that went wrong and the power of seeing all the things that were going right. I used to bombard myself with tasks, deadlines, and busy work to feel a sense of accomplishment and progress. I have since learned the importance of my morning routine and the power I have to set the tone for my day.

Every morning, it is my mission to get myself into a powerful state; a state where I feel focused, relaxed, energized and purpose driven. I am no longer a victim to circumstance but a believer that you get out what you put in. If you sow negative thoughts, you will harvest negative results. If you withhold from fully giving yourself to your goals, then you will experience limited fulfillment. The biggest change I see about my progress is the way I view my mission. I used to work to get the result as fast as possible. I now work to get a result in a way that is sustainable.

REFLECTIONS:

After reading this passage, I realize:

Affirmation: *I have access to the best things in life. Joy, peace, passion and purpose live within me.*

Questions to process:

What habits do I need to change to get to the next level on my journey?

Why is this important to me?

After answering the questions above, I now understand:

Moving forward, I will:

Beliefs That Create or Eliminate the Possibilities That Live in Your Future

You get to choose what is possible in your life. I didn't always understand this. I often felt like the road was chosen for me and I needed to rise to the occasion in order to prove to others that I was worth knowing. The importance of education was drilled into me early on. As a child, I understood that I had to go to school in order to have a promising future.

Life experience has taught me that while being educated is important, going to school is *not* the only way to build a life I feel proud of. There are people who go to school and fail to apply themselves. Some struggle with maintaining consistent study habits, focus, discipline, support and responsibility. School and certifications do not define your future, you do! Although school and certifications have many great benefits (i.e. access to thought leaders and their journeys, different kinds of people, new experiences, etc.), there are a few things that I have come to realize about the way we are educated.

First, we spend a good portion of our lives going to school. In school, we receive instructions and expectations and get graded on how well someone else believes we have followed the instructions or met the expectations. This method has a great impact on our belief in ourselves and our abilities to create the lives that we truly desire. We are conditioned to seek the approval of others and to look outward about matters regarding the things we intrinsically value most. Many of us struggle with believing in ourselves because we have grown dependent upon external affirmation.

I'm here to tell you that school and certifications alone don't make you competent or successful. There are so many stories of phenomenal people who have done amazing things in their lives without certifications or traditional schooling. Some components of living a fulfilled life are choosing to: meet new people, create new experiences, learn something new, read books and be open to feedback.

Next, I always thought that school guaranteed success. The truth is that the choices you make, habits you develop, and attitudes you maintain determine your future. Whether pursuing school or life experiences, the choice is yours and there is no right way to build a life that you feel proud of. What is important is that you make the choice to be a lifelong learner. Invest in your dreams. Use every opportunity to become your best! Visualize, make a plan, take action, reflect and repeat. School is an investment that I am grateful for but it did *not* make me successful. School was not the source of my success, but a resource I chose to take me to the next level. You have the power to choose!

Reflections:

After reading this passage, I realize:

Affirmation: *I have everything I need to create the life my soul longs for. I will allow myself to envision a life I feel good about. I am capable of making the necessary decisions to create this life.*

Questions to process:

What do I need to believe in order to build a life I feel proud of?

Why is this belief important?

After answering the questions above, I now understand:

Moving forward, I will:

Trust Your Process

It has taken some time but life has taught me to trust my own process. Many times, when we see others get results, we ask them, "How did you do it?," seeking their blueprint, hoping it will work for us. We try it, fail, get discouraged, ask someone else about their process and repeat the cycle without taking into account that what works for others may not work for us. We are different people, with varying motivations, preferences, processes and life circumstances.

When you set a goal, set it from a place in your mind where you've already accomplished it and create your own plan to do so. Once you create your plan, commit 100 percent. Don't settle for excuses, don't compare your process to others and firmly believe in the actions *you* are taking to get the results you desire.

Truth is, there is a process that works for you. It's *your* process. In order to perfect it, you must be aware of your fears, strengths, thoughts, feelings, behaviors, limitations and growth areas. These key factors impact your ability to create and sustain your plan. Before creating a plan, it's important to know how you work so you can create a plan that works for you. Self-awareness is key to creating a sustainable lifestyle.

Reflections:

After reading this passage, I realize:

Affirmation: *I can achieve my goals by becoming more self-aware and creating a process that works for me.*

Questions to process:

How has self-awareness helped me meet my goals?

What puts, and keeps me, in the zone?

After answering the questions above, I now understand:

Moving forward, I will:

You Are Meant for More

There have been so many times in my life where I have played it small: desiring to be seen, heard and cared for, and yet deeply afraid of rejection. I didn't want to be perceived as needy. I didn't want to feel unwanted. I didn't fully understand that it is my birthright to be seen, heard and cared for. The problem was that I was seeking a sense of belonging from those who didn't have the capacity to see me, hear me, or care for me in the ways I deserve.

Once I did the work to see, hear and care for myself, I learned that I am meant to have more. I am meant to have more fulfilling and energizing relationships. I am meant to have more time to rest and relax. I am meant to have more opportunities to feel loved and appreciated. I am meant to enjoy more laughter and peace. I am meant to cultivate more meaningful interactions. I am meant to engage in more of what makes me feel alive!

And, so are you! You are meant for so much more than you are settling for. So walk courageously and live boldly and confidently. Believe in your ability to journey down your unique path in a way that feels life-giving to you!

Reflections:

After reading this passage I realize:

Affirmation: *I will live a big life and journey down my unique path in a way that feels life-giving to me!*

Questions to process:

In what ways have I played it small in my life?

What contributed to me playing it small?

After answering the questions above, I now understand:

Moving forward, I will:

Being In the Driver's Seat In Your Life

How are driving and becoming your best-self related?

Both require you to identify where you are and where you want to go. Having a vision for your life is essential to reaching your destination.

You get to choose how to get there. There are many routes you can choose but you must be clear of what is important to you as you venture out. Do you prefer the scenic route? Does the amount of time it takes to get there matter more? Does traffic bother you? The clearer you are about what matters to you, the easier it will become to choose what route you want to take.

You must keep going in order to reach the desired destination. You will not reach your destination if you refuse to move forward. No matter how many times you stop or reroute, continuing to move forward toward the destination is key.

Keep your eyes on the road ahead. Pay attention and don't lose sight of where you're heading. You may experience roadblocks, detours, accidents and winding roads, but you are strong enough to get past these temporary setbacks. Stay the course and keep looking ahead.

You have to look in the mirror to see your blind spots and adjust accordingly. Having support as you journey is important. Know the supports around you and allow them to assist you when needed.

You may encounter detours, but remember that you can always be rerouted. The route can change as long as the destination remains the same.

You need to maintain distance between you and others. This allows you to gain perspective and maintain mental and emotional control while on your journey.

Resist speeding. It puts you at a higher risk of losing control and you'll have less time to notice and react to unexpected situations.

Combat fatigue by taking breaks for longer distances and making sure you rest. Understand what makes you tired, have a plan for rest and implement the plan as often as needed.

Know your limits. Boundaries help you keep in what is good and keep out the bad. Proceed with caution and take heed of the things that may cause you to crash.

Stay in your lane. Everyone around you has their own destination. You are only responsible for what takes place in the car you are driving.

Don't forget to refuel. You can't go anywhere empty. Self-care is a must.

Becoming your best self doesn't have to be a cross country trip. Simply buckle up and enjoy the ride.

Reflections:

After reading this passage, I realize:

Affirmation: *I am in the driver's seat in my life. I know where I am and where I want to go. I will continue to move forward and reach my destination.*

Questions to process:

What does my best self look like? (What am I doing? How am I feeling? What am I learning? What am I accomplishing?)

What can I do today to refuel?

After answering the questions above, I now understand:

Moving forward, I will:

Doing Whatever It Takes to Become Your Best

You have to be willing to do whatever it takes to become who you want to be. In order to become your best, you have to get to the other side of who you currently are. That requires change; change in how you: think and what you choose to focus on, how you allow yourself to fully feel, without resistance, and your habits.

Change requires more than just creating a goal or routine. It requires more than telling yourself you can do it and feeling motivated. It all starts in your mind. What are you telling yourself about who you want to be and why?

Change is maintained by your consistency of thought. You have to decide every moment if the choices you are making serve your best self. It takes willingness to complete the necessary actions required to get to the next level. You must change how you see yourself and act accordingly.

Envision who you would be once you become your best self. What would you be doing? Who would you be doing it with? How would you dress? What thoughts would you think? What feelings would you feel? Start showing up like that now.

Say "no" to easy options. Get clear about what you want and don't settle for anything less. The only person who can stop you from becoming your best self is *you*! You can do this. Take the first step.

Reflections:

After reading this passage, I realize:

Affirmation: *I will get to the other side of my current situation. I will become the best version of myself.*

Questions to process:

What instant gratification is currently stopping me from becoming my best self?

How can I stop giving into it in order to reap the long term results of my goals?

After answering the questions above, I now understand:

Moving forward, I will:

The Power of Belief and Taking Action

In December of 2020, I quit my job, submitted my notice to vacate my apartment, disenrolled my kids from school and set my sights to relocate to another state. The week before we were supposed to move, I decided not to. I did not have peace and discovered some truths about this move that were unsettling.

When I realized that I was not relocating, I didn't ask the landlord to reconsider my notice. I didn't ask my former employer for my job back. The truth was that I did not like my place of residence, nor my employer. I wasn't satisfied with my quality of life. Overall, we were in the middle of the pandemic. Many people were facing unemployment.

When January came, I had a month to find a new job and a new home for my family. I was clear about what I wanted: a job where I could unapologetically be myself, to invest in the Black community, partner with a rockstar boss who didn't micro-manage me and the opportunity to create a national best practice model. Even though job opportunities were at an all time low, it only took me two short weeks to find an employer that checked all of my boxes.

When identifying a new home, I was clear that I wanted to live in a family-oriented community, be very close to child-centered activities, and have four bedrooms with a very specific type of refrigerator. With a terrible credit score and all the hope and belief in the world, I obtained housing within those same two weeks. Your dream may not make sense. You may not meet all of the requirements. You may not even qualify, but do it anyway. I believed when the evidence proved this was nearly "impossible," and now "impossible" has become my reality.

I wrote my goals and desires and went to work to achieve them. I stayed up all night looking for private owners who would give me a chance. I spent more than eight hours a day looking for suitable jobs, tweaking my resume, writing cover letters and submitting applications. I drove from open house to open house, receiving rejection after rejection due to my low credit score. But, I didn't give up. No matter how many "no's" were presented, I kept my mind focused on the one "yes" I needed to make my goal a reality.

It seemed as if all the odds were stacked against me. When I would share my vision with those close to me, they looked at me questionably. But, I was relentless in my pursuit to get to the other side of my situation. I didn't care about others' thoughts and opinions.

I didn't live in the fear of rejection. I didn't stand in a mindset of scarcity. I stood in *belief*, knowing that if I continued to show up for what I wanted, it would show up. And, it did. The evidence of standing firm in that belief has given me the ability to hold space and belief for even bigger dreams that are currently becoming reality.

No matter how difficult it may seem, you can build the life that you want. The only requirement is that you must be willing to do the work!

Reflections:

After reading this passage, I realize:

Affirmation: *I can hold space for believing in the impossible. I can be the evidence of what is possible and create a path many have never walked.*

Questions to process:

With what areas of my life am I currently dissatisfied?

Why do I remain in these spaces?

After answering the questions above, I now understand:

Moving forward, I will:

Building Credibility With Yourself

Honoring your word is so important. When you say you're going to do something, make sure you do it. It's easy to get caught up in how others are affected by your decisions. Although it is important to consider others, what's even more important is recognizing how breaking your commitments to yourself affects you. When you fail to keep commitments to yourself, it creates internal criticism such as negative self-talk, a skewed perception of yourself and negative feelings that all chip away at trust.

If you are human, you have failed to keep a commitment at some point in time. Most times, the broken commitment is unintentional. Breaking a commitment is not detrimental in and of itself. But how we choose to respond to it is.

Therefore, if you desire to stay positively connected to yourself by keeping your word, it is helpful to do the following: write down any commitments that you make, say "no" if a request has been made that you can't fully commit to, carve out time in your schedule to fulfill the commitment and communicate as soon as you find out you won't be able to honor your commitments. Following these steps will help alleviate the guilt and shame when you can't follow through. This way, you can still be intentional and show up, even if it is not in the way you originally desired to.

Consistently keeping your word builds confidence, develops trust, generates a standard and demonstrates self-respect.

As you evaluate your current life situation, you will find that all you have was built on a series of commitments you've made. Your place of residence is based on a commitment to pay rent or mortgage. Any degrees, certifications or places of employment have been obtained based on time commitments. The more you look, the more you will find how essential commitments are in your life.

Please don't look back at broken commitments from the past. Rather, look forward, start again and rebuild credibility with yourself. You'll be glad you did.

Reflections:

After reading this passage, I realize:

Affirmation: *I will honor my commitments, especially to myself. I will keep my commitments and provide myself with the trust I am seeking.*

Questions to process:

What commitments would I like to make?

Why are they important to me?

After answering the questions above, I now understand:

Moving forward, I will:

Boundaries Start With You

For a long time, I lived without boundaries, constantly critiquing others and blaming them for their lack of regard for me. Then one day, it clicked. People were only mirroring what I modeled. People were also treating me in the ways I allowed myself to be treated. In hindsight, if I wanted to feel respected, I first needed to figure out what it meant to respect myself. Then, I needed to get clear about my expectations of others.

When creating limits that work for you, it is important to get clear about your values, beliefs, wants, needs and deal breakers. Without this understanding, you will continue to: put the needs and feelings of others before your own, say "yes" to things you wish you hadn't, spend a lot of time wondering what others are thinking about you and give away too much of your time. When you take the time to create and honor boundaries, you will create a space to freely: say "no" without feeling guilty, engage in self-care without feeling selfish, have clarity about what you want and need and maintain healthy relationships with yourself and others. This will enable you to live life on your terms.

You may be asking yourself, "So how do I create boundaries?" A good place to start is by gaining an understanding about the purpose of boundaries. You need to stop ignoring your thoughts, feelings and needs and explore them. You need to think through how you want to spend your time and energy. Become clear about the types of communication and behaviors you will allow. Create a morning or night routine and stick to them. Practice saying "no" from an authentic place. Remember, you are not responsible for the thoughts and feelings of others. You are only responsible for your own.

Some people may not like when you begin to establish new boundaries because they were the ones who benefited from your lack of boundaries in the first place. People will only treat you the way you allow them to treat you. More importantly, the way you treat yourself demonstrates how you want others to treat you. Don't be afraid to set boundaries. It will only bring in more of what you want and help you to let go of what you don't.

Reflections:

After reading this passage, I realize:

Affirmation: ***I am worthy of creating boundaries that keep me safe and secure. I can ask for what I need and expect, without feeling guilty or ashamed.***

Questions to process:

What boundaries do I currently have in place?

What new boundaries do I need to develop and with whom?

After answering the questions above, I now understand:

Moving forward, I will:

Getting Results With Consistency and Intentionality

I remember sitting in the doctor's office for a check-up. The doctor asked how I was feeling and if I had been feeling anything out of the norm. I wondered why she was asking me all of these unfamiliar questions. I was four months pregnant with my youngest son when I was informed that I had high blood pressure.

I never had any health issues before, " I asked myself how could this be happening? Before I could get a word out, the doctor asked if I understood what that meant and told me I'd be on medication for the rest of my life. I was beyond frustrated to say the least. Who gives someone news like that without providing options and remedies first?

I was convinced that my high blood pressure was due to being pregnant. I believed it would just go away once I had my son. Unfortunately, once I had him, my blood pressure was the same–still high! It didn't help that I continued to eat fast food regularly, resisted working out, mindlessly ate and inconsistently tracked my blood pressure.

This went on for months, until I had to go to the emergency room. I remember having migraines, laying in a dark room with sunglasses on for hours, experiencing heart palpitations and not being able to see. When I went to my follow-up appointment with my primary doctor, we created a plan to lower my blood pressure. When I left the office, I was determined to overcome this new health challenge. This diagnosis wasn't going to define me and the doctor certainly didn't have the final say.

I started to eat better, exercise more, log my salt intake, regularly check my blood pressure and follow a routine that energized me and put me in an empowering mindset. I was reminded that consistency is an essential component to accomplishing goals and would produce the results I desired. I was in a hard place, but I knew what needed to be done to walk in freedom and I did it. You can too. Now, get to it!

Reflections:

After reading this passage, I realize:

Affirmation: *I can stick to my plans and create the results I want in life.*

Questions to process:

What am I currently determined to overcome?

What have I done to try and overcome this?

After answering the questions above, I now understand:

Moving forward, I will:

Invest in You

We all have priorities. Some of us accomplish them by creating to-do lists, utilizing planners, or putting reminders on calendars. Even though we are aware of our priorities, we usually put our priorities in the "whenever I get to it" category. We more readily prioritize work, family and friendships, rarely carving out time for ourselves.

We begin to convince ourselves that "our time" is driving alone in the car, cleaning the house when no one is around, going grocery shopping, running errands alone or completing a task for the greater good. This used to be my mindset. Due to my limited beliefs about self-care, it took my health to be compromised in order for me to prioritize quality time with myself. It took time for me to learn how to identify things that give my life meaning and make me happy. I had to do better with monitoring my eating. I had to make time to exercise and center myself in prayer and silence.

Once I began to create a routine around things I enjoy, I began to feel stronger and more energized. I could then care for others better, operate with patience, focus for longer periods of time and sleep better. This lived experience made the saying, "You can't pour from an empty cup" became very real for me. I had to figure out how to fill myself up.

There are many ways to do this. Some carve out fifteen minutes of the day to walk, journal, pray, exercise, sit in silence, meal prep or give thanks. There are so many meaningful ways to engage with yourself. Invest in you. Make self-care a standard in your life and watch how things begin to change for the better!

Reflections:

After reading this passage, I realize:

Affirmation: *I will make self-care a standard in my life.*

Questions to process:

How will pouring into myself benefit me?

If I don't pour into myself, how could this negatively impact me?

After answering the questions above, I now understand:

Moving forward, I will:

Centered in Self-Care

What do you think about when you hear "self-care"? Some people think of self-care as taking lavish vacations and trips to the spa, spending money unnecessarily, or being selfish and doing grand things. Here's what it means to me: making healthy choices for your mental, physical, emotional, spiritual, financial, professional, parental, and relational maturity. Self-care is also setting goals, creating boundaries, establishing routines and introspection. You honor yourself when you honor your choices and commitments and communicate your needs.

There's a difference between being self-centered and being centered-in-self. For instance, self-centered people are: entitled, lack empathy, struggle with superiority, use people, tend to be superficial, expect to be catered to and believe the world revolves around them. Whereas, people who are centered in themselves are balanced, peaceful, accepting, compassionate, emotionally regulated, connected to their feelings, in control of their thoughts and actions, self-aware, reflective and not easily influenced by others.

Self-care is more about being centered in yourself, rather than having everything be centered around you. Make it a habit to set aside time to recharge and give yourself what you need.

Reflections:

After reading this passage, I realize:

Affirmation: *I will become centered in myself and give myself what I need consistently and unapologetically.*

Questions to process:

How do I define self-care?

What does it look like for me to get centered in myself?

After answering the questions above, I now understand:

Moving forward, I will:

Ask For What You Need

Don't let fear of rejection, the appearance of having it all together or limited beliefs about strength rob you from getting your needs met. The greatest thing you can do is advocate for yourself. We don't have what we want or need because we don't ask. We are human and we all have needs.

So, make that vacation request. Take a mental health day. Ask someone to clarify what they mean. See a coach or a counselor. Set boundaries. Hire that house cleaner. Request that extension and know that you are worthy of carving out time for yourself.

Reflections:

After reading this passage, I realize:

Affirmation: ***Asking for what I need is one of my greatest strengths.***

Questions to process:

What do I need to ask for that I haven't yet?

What is keeping me from asking?

After answering the questions above, I now understand:

Moving forward, I will:

Envisioning and Creating Your Desired Life

We all dream about living a fulfilling life. We imagine that when we are fulfilled we will have peace and enough time in the day to do what we want. We will have balance, confidence and self-love. We will be healthy in every area of our lives. The tangible things we desire most are meaningful work, healthy relationships, healthy finances, a healthy mindset and a healthy body.

Although we have an idea of the life we want, we find ourselves struggling to figure out what to do in order to make these ideas a reality. Identifying my life's mission, vision, values and goals has inspired me to take action. I had to find something to do that felt meaningful and important. I had to develop the discipline to ask myself a series of questions and also create space to answer these questions from the most genuine place within myself.

I challenged myself by continuously assessing and reevaluating my thoughts, feelings and behaviors. I wrote motivating notes on my phone, empowering quotes on sticky notes and listened to music and podcasts that inspired me to keep moving forward. I wrote my goals as if they already happened. Everyday, I recited how grateful I was to have everything I've always wanted. I continued to do this until I finally did. I took inventory of what I most enjoy doing in my free time when no one is around. I started paying attention to things I naturally found interesting and things I wanted to learn more about. I asked myself, "*What do I find myself talking about the most? What issue am I passionate about solving? How do I want people to remember me when I am no longer here?*

These thoughts and questions helped move me into a space where I felt clear and inspired. It was from this place that I began to create an action plan, outlining what I desired to accomplish and a timeline for getting it done.

I encourage you to take some time to sit with yourself and become clear about where you would like to be in the next five to ten years. What do you want to feel? Who do you want around you? What would you like to accomplish? When are you going to begin allowing yourself to work and create experiences that align with your desires?

Reflections:

After reading this passage, I realize:

Affirmation: ***I will create the necessary time to envision and create the life I was meant to live. I will get clear about my passions and goals and I will do what's necessary to make them come true.***

Questions to process:

What do I want to accomplish in life?

What obstacles are stopping me?

After answering the questions above, I now understand:

Moving forward, I will:

Start Living Your Dream

Deep inside all of us is a desire to live a meaningful life. There is something within us that the world needs to witness and something we long to see in the world. The problem is, many of us struggle to figure out what that is and how to manifest it. I asked myself: "*What does my life currently mean? What do I want it to mean? What am I spending the majority of my energy on? What am I giving most of my time to? Am I allocating time daily to engage with, or in, the things that matter the most to me? Am I merely living or am I creating a fulfilled life? What do I desire to accomplish before my time on Earth expires?*"

I had to journey through the hard questions to find the truth about what I value most. When answering these questions, I realized I love helping others fulfill their wildest dreams. I want to accomplish self-mastery, live a balanced life and show people what is possible when they show up for themselves. I had to deal with the reality that my mindset was the main obstacle that prevented me from taking the steps to living my ideal life.

Honestly, I didn't truly believe I could build the life I desired. I was afraid of what people would say if I showed up authentically as myself. What if I did it wrong? Or, even worse, failed? What if people wouldn't like me? Where would I go from here?

I had to study myself, be honest with myself, forgive myself, and truly learn to like and love myself. Up until this point, every version of myself needed to be loved, acknowledged and appreciated. So, I got clear about my life mission, started to set goals and worked everyday to become more consistent and disciplined. I started to view everyday as a new opportunity to make myself proud and work to maintain an attitude of gratitude.

I learned that achieving my dreams is a daily process of being willing to do whatever it takes to meet my goals.

Suggestions to help you meet your goals:

- Create an environment that will get you into a healthy headspace.
- Create an intentional schedule and commit to it.
- Each night, before bed, reflect and evaluate how the day went to help you better prepare for the days ahead.

I had to set an intention in order to live out my vision and here I am. So, I ask you, "When will you begin to live your dream? What will you accomplish with your life? What steps will you take to get there? What do you need to address in order to begin building the life you want?" Never forget that your life has meaning. Do the work to get your message out and show people what's possible!

Reflections:

After reading this passage, I realize:

Affirmation: *Every version of me is worthy of being acknowledged, appreciated and loved. I will love who I've been, who I am and who I'm becoming.*

Questions to process:

What intentions do I need to set in order to live out the vision for my life?

What do I need to do daily in order to be proud of myself every night before I go to bed?

After answering the questions above, I now understand:

Moving forward, I will:

Push Past Hard Things With Belief

I have many vivid memories of experiencing great laughter and excitement with my dad. His laugh was contagious and his energy magnetic. He made me feel like I could do anything in this life. He loved wholeheartedly and was always full of surprises; some, not so pleasant. Many times, he would tell me and my brother that he was coming to see us and take us somewhere fun. We would get dressed, wait on him for hours, only to feel deeply disappointed when he didn't show up. Everytime we asked him why he didn't come, he would say, "Something came up."

Over the years, I consistently witnessed my dad in and out of jail, drunk, and homeless. His failures became more and more apparent the older I got. I remember being so confused because everytime he got out of jail he instantly got a job. I wondered, "Can you get a job after going to jail this many times?" Over time, I began to ask him how he always found a place to work. He'd always say, "C'mon, it's me. Don't worry about me, I'm gonna always be okay." What I didn't know, but learned in my teenage years, was that my father struggled with drug and alcohol addiction. But no matter how many times he fell, I watched him get back up.

I've come to realize how deeply his belief was instilled in me. Time and experience have revealed to me that his message and resilience gifted me with grit, grace, and the belief that I will always make it to the other side of my situation. This mindset that "no matter what, I can always show up for my dreams and I will always be okay," is what gave me the courage to: pursue my education, live in several states across the country, try on different career titles, cut off toxic relationships, become a parent and start my own business.

Now that I am a parent, I often find myself "trying on my dad's shoes." I wonder what beliefs helped him overcome his addiction, admit his struggles to my brother and I, ask for forgiveness and consistently speak life into me, no matter what. The thought fills me with so much strength, compassion, positivity and gratitude. I inherited the power of his confidence and now have the gift of believing so deeply not only in myself, but in the capabilities of others to accomplish hard things.

Sometimes we don't understand things as they are happening to us, but the lessons begin to make sense with time. Even in hard times, you have the power to make connections that give your life and experience more meaning.

Reflections:

After reading this passage, I realize:

Affirmation: *I will always show up for my dreams. I will always believe in myself. I will always be okay, no matter what happens.*

Questions to process:

Who has given me the gift of believing? When? How?

What experiences have taught me that no matter what I will be okay?

After answering the questions above, I now understand:

Moving forward, I will:

Allow Your Knowledge to Fuel Your Actions

Stop watching everyone else live their lives and start building yours. Invest in yourself. Make sure you are okay. Identify and embrace your imperfections. Create an inspiring routine. Forgive yourself and others. Encourage yourself. Intentionally carve out daily alone time. Self-reflect. Explore a new place. Go through old pictures, scrapbooks and journals and reflect on your growth.

At a minimum, find ways to incorporate celebrating yourself weekly. Find a creative outlet. Learn to say "no." Start a DIY project. Tell others what you need. Take a nap. Take yourself on a date. Write yourself a love letter. Go for a walk or run. Allow yourself to cry. Say aloud what you are grateful for. Ask for help. Go to counseling. Set boundaries. Slow down. Find balance. Write out everything that's on your mind.

The most important thing you can do is get out of your head and get into action. Do whatever you need to do to reset, recharge and refocus so you can push ahead with clarity, purpose, and fulfillment. Many of us are stagnant because we refuse to change or challenge our thinking, question our feelings and try something new. Change doesn't happen because you verbally say you need to change. Change begins when you allow yourself to think, feel and *do* something differently.

Reflections:

After reading this passage I realize:

Affirmation: *I am resetting, refocusing and recharging to push ahead with clarity, purpose and fulfillment.*

Questions to process:

What most excites me about this passage?

What, from this passage, do I most look forward to doing?

After answering the questions above, I now understand:

Moving forward, I will:

Permission to be Vulnerable

Throughout my life, I have often been affirmed for being strong and independent. Many people have said, "I don't worry about you because I know you'll figure it out." Because of this, I found myself showing up for everyone else, but felt alone when faced with the darker moments in my life. I often wondered why no one showed up for me. Then, one day, it hit me. No one showed up for me because I wouldn't allow them. Honestly, I didn't really know how to show up for myself.

I had been called strong for so long that I didn't realize how much of my identity depended upon that perception. My strength was my shield. It protected me from criticism, rejection, shame and embarrassment. It was so much easier to lean into being strong than to face my fear of being misunderstood and ignored, until I got tired of being strong.

I began to realize how much energy it took to continue "saving the day" and I realized being "strong" and "independent" was keeping me from what I truly desired: intimacy with others, unconditional love and acceptance, being seen, heard, and understood and simply being.

I began to process why I struggled so badly with being vulnerable. I noticed that vulnerability was not modeled to me growing up. I had a skewed perception of vulnerability and didn't feel comfortable enough with myself to reveal my insecurities to others. I didn't know how to cope with my hurt feelings and disappointments. It eventually became clear that in order to grow, I must learn to let others in, embrace my humanity, and learn to ask for what I need, trusting I'd be okay if I didn't get the desired response.

Before I could achieve the growth I desired, I first needed to learn more about my needs, wants, and coping patterns. I needed to face my fears and give myself the opportunity to strengthen my vulnerability muscle. I began to ask myself hard questions and created ways to challenge myself to grow emotionally. I gave myself permission to be vulnerable with others. Now, I feel connected to people in a way that feels life-giving. Vulnerability *is* a strength and it is one of the ingredients to creating a life seeped in authenticity.

Reflections:

After reading this passage, I realize:

Affirmation: *I will allow myself to be seen, heard and understood. I will allow myself to be vulnerable.*

Questions to process:

What insecurities am I trying to conceal from others?

How are others' perceptions of me affecting my self-perception?

After answering the questions above, I now understand:

Moving forward, I will:

The Prescription

In my early life, I learned that if I shared how I *really* felt I would upset others and make them either reject me, or angry with me. Somewhere along my journey, I mastered keeping others happy and interested in me by prioritizing their feelings over mine. Instead of addressing toxic behaviors or acknowledging my feelings or expressing my emotional needs, I would take 20mg of denial. It kept me from experiencing feelings of stress, anxiety, overwhelm and deep pain.

This medication provided me with the pleasure of living in my imagination instead of reality. Over time, I became addicted to seeing only what I wanted to see instead of what was actually in front of me. I was an expert at finding ways to overlook issues that made me uncomfortable. I often found myself justifying the things I was afraid to confront by telling myself that no matter what I said or did, it "wouldn't make a difference." The more I prioritized others, the less I experienced true love, joy, gratitude and self-care. Denial was chipping away at the greatest part of me and I knew change was essential.

So, how does one stop operating in denial? I had to honestly examine my fear. I began the process of accepting and expressing my emotions. I had to think about what would happen if I continued to operate this way and the impacts it would have on my life. Then I had to create a plan to stop using denial to avoid pain and learn how to process pain while accepting the truth.

I began to journal about the worst case scenarios of the fears that lived within asking myself "What triggers these fears?" I had to sit with the discomfort and figure out where these fears showed up within my body. I had to identify thoughts and feelings associated with these fears. Then, I'd write down everything that came up for me as I considered these things. I had to go deep in order to discover the false narrative I was believing around these fears.

I got curious about why I didn't feel I could overcome them. I committed to having hard conversations not only with myself but with those closest to me. I began to tell myself and others how I felt, the behaviors I didn't like, and what I wanted and needed. In the beginning, this felt terrible because it felt so foreign. Over time, it has become a natural part of who I am.

Although denial provides temporary relief from pain, facing the truth has given me the ability to have hard conversations, be grateful for my feelings and to know my worth– even if others refuse to see it. You don't have to deny your thoughts and feelings in order to keep the peace. Peace comes with honestly sharing your truth.

Reflections:

After reading this passage, I realize:

Affirmation: *Telling my truth will allow me to experience true love, joy, gratitude and self-care.*

Questions to process:

Do I deal with negative emotions, or "protect" myself from them? How? Why?

What do I need to learn in order to tell the truth and maintain my peace?

After answering the questions above, I now understand:

Moving forward, I will:

Growth

Five pregnancies and three children later, I found myself in the *worst* shape of my life. I'm not sure how I got there, but I know it started with the belief that in order for me to be a good mother and wife, I had to come last. My mind and body took the biggest hit. I experienced migraines, body aches, heavy breathing, and overall exhaustion.

How did this former athlete let herself go? This question lived in my mind for months, but it didn't stop me from continuing unhealthy habits like overeating, not exercising, making excuses and feeling sorry for myself. When the new year rolled around, I was ready! I didn't want to wake up another day not recognizing myself, having low energy, being embarrassed about the way I looked or loathing shopping for myself.

I made it my goal to put myself first because self-care is not selfish, it's essential. I had to change my belief about what it took to be my best self, which included being a great mom, wife and my own person. I signed up for the gym and attended the five o'clock in the morning class, four times a week, no matter what. I changed my eating habits and used an app to track my meals. I drank more than a half a gallon of water daily. I listened to motivational podcasts and joined groups that consisted of other women sharing their weight loss milestones.

So far, I have lost forty pounds! I remind myself that I go to the gym daily because it's what my body needs and I like the way it makes me feel, physically and mentally. The weight loss is the cherry on top. Putting myself first has been the best decision I have made in a long time. I show up better for my family, with colleagues, friends, and most importantly, for myself. You don't have to sacrifice yourself for the greater good. When you are good, greater is inevitable.

Reflections:

After reading this passage, I realize:

Affirmation: *Putting myself first is essential to my personal growth and the growth of everything around me.*

Questions to process:

What habits are keeping me from becoming better?

What will I gain from leaving this habit behind?

After answering the questions above, I now understand:

Moving forward, I will:

Rejection is Not a Reflection of Me

Five to ten years ago, my main priority was getting a good job. I remember preparing for interviews, hoping I was "good enough" for the position. I would go into an interview filled with nerves and anxiety, hoping I'd say the right things and be selected for the job. Since then, I have learned to not allow others' rejection be a reflection of me. Just because someone doesn't pick me doesn't mean I am not worthy. It simply means they either can't see my worth, or desire something else.

I now know that the goal isn't to be liked or seen as competent. The goal is to simply exude my confidence and share my competence. Rather than walking into interviews and wondering, "Am I what they're looking for?" I ask myself, "Are they what I'm looking for?" I am clear about who I am and how I operate. I will not tolerate micro-managing, toxic cultures or time stamps. I know how to utilize my strengths and leverage the skills of my team to support me in the areas in which they thrive.

If I could talk to my younger self, I would say, "Be clear about what you are looking for. What do you want? Why does it matter? How does it align with your future? Don't wait for someone to choose you. Pick where you want to be and do the work to get there."

Now, I say the same to you. Get clear about what you want, why you want it and how it brings you closer to becoming your best self. Then, get to work! You've got this! If you don't believe you do, then I'm more than happy to be your corrective lens so that you can clearly see just how great you really are! You can do this and I know you will!

Reflections:

After reading this passage, I realize:

Affirmation: *I am a reflection of strength, possibility and determination. I will exude competence and confidence, regardless of others' judgments of me.*

Questions to process:

How do I deal with rejection? What meaning do I attach to my responses?

What have I tolerated in the past, from myself and others, that I won't any longer?

After answering the questions above, I now understand:

Moving forward, I will:

Choose What's in Your Best Interest

Many of us have functioned on auto pilot, or in survival mode for so long that we've lost touch with the things that make us feel alive. We desire to live our dream, but can't seem to figure out how. More times than not, we rob ourselves of the opportunity to be our best because we don't believe it's possible. We are afraid of what others might think or feel. We aren't willing to do what it takes to be great.

Truth is, whether you work to be great or not, you will fail. You can fail by choosing not to try, or by facing the inevitable when trying something new. You can succeed at staying the same or going to the next level. You can lose happiness because of your resistance to change, or lose old habits that were holding you back. You can hurt in the long-term, wallowing in the pain of what could have been. Or, hurt temporarily because of the habits you have to give up to move forward. You can judge yourself because you know you are capable of so much more. Or, be judged by others because you are modeling what more actually looks like. You can be afraid of the possibilities and settle for a mediocre life. Or, fear living another day feeling stuck and do what it takes to get unstuck.

My love, don't be afraid of becoming the best person possible. Prioritize yourself. Believe you can become better. Push yourself to learn. Focus on improvement. Wake up everyday with the mission to grow. Live a meaningful life. You can do hard things. It all starts with a choice. Choose growth and you won't regret it.

Reflections:

After reading this passage, I realize:

Affirmation: *I choose to wake up everyday with a mission to grow. I will blossom into the person I know I'm supposed to be.*

Questions to process:

What will help me grow right now, right where I am?

What can I do right now to make sure I continue to grow?

After answering the questions above, I now understand:

Moving forward, I will:

Live Anyway

Many of us have our minds set on unrealistic time tables. I often make suggestions to clients about growth opportunities and hear, "I'm too old for that." Or, "I should know this by now." So many people are walking around with loads of shame, regrets and fears because they are paralyzed by beliefs about their age.

Some people believe they should be married and have kids by a certain age. Others believe their chances at love have expired because they didn't find the connection they wanted while in their "prime." Some people stay in toxic relationships because they believe they are too old to start dating again and refuse to be alone.

I've witnessed people with weight loss goals who have chosen to tolerate a body they don't desire because they believe they are too old for a workout routine. I've worked with people who desire to go back to school but feel they aren't young enough to be in college. I've spoken to people that stay at dead end jobs because they think they are too old for a career change. I've encountered people who are embarrassed to admit that they struggle with prioritizing themselves and setting healthy boundaries because they feel they should know better by now.

I'm here to tell you that you're never too old and it's never too late to do things that make you feel proud. Don't let age determine your fitness goals, relationship status, level of education or place of employment. The amount of time you are alive doesn't compare to the amount of time you spend living. Get out there, and start living and stop merely existing! You have dreams to make into a reality. Get to work!

Reflections:

After reading this passage, I realize:

Affirmation: *I determine who I am and what I will become in my life. My choices are what determine my future and I will choose wisely.*

Questions to process:

In what ways have I allowed my age to discourage me from accomplishing my goals?

What do I believe I should know by now that I don't? What can I do to learn these things?

After answering the questions above, I now understand:

Moving forward, I will:

Let it Go

The only way to get what you really want is to let go of what you don't want. At first, I thought I had to be clear about what I wanted in order to begin letting things go. The truth is, I became much clearer about what I wanted once I began to let go of what I didn't. Goodbye instability, inactivity, unhappiness, criticism, limitations, toxicity, inconsistency, restlessness, procrastination and negativity. Once I said "goodbye," it freed me up to say "hello" to things I truly desired. Now, I must determine how I can develop the capacity to hold the things I truly want.

Reflections:

After reading this passage, I realize:

Affirmation: *I am letting go of what doesn't serve me to make room for what does.*

Questions to process:

What do I need to let go of?

How long have I held on to these things and what purpose have they served?

After answering the questions above, I now understand:

Moving forward, I will:

Walk in Truth

There's a truth inside all of us waiting to be uncovered. What is yours? We all crave the truth, but fear it simultaneously, because of the feelings it brings up when we get clear about what is going on inside, and around, us. Fear is an illusion. It is not true. Usually, the things we fear the most are the worst case scenarios we attach to any given situation. For example, some will tell you that they are afraid of the dark. Truth is no one is afraid of the dark. The fear comes from what we believe exists in the dark, whether it be the boogie man, a thief, or any other negative possibility.

We will never get to the other side of our fears until we face them. We will only come to know what's in the dark when we turn on the light and investigate for ourselves. Once we choose to do this, the next step is to believe that we can handle whatever is found. Then comes the work of actually connecting your skills to the revealed situation. Some of us lack the tools to individually deal with what we find in the dark. We need the support of someone to: hold belief for us when we don't have eyes to see, hold space for us as we process and allow us to simply be safe. Don't be afraid of the truth. Learn to walk in it and ask for support along the way.

Reflections:

After reading this passage, I realize:

Affirmation: *I am strong enough to face the truth.*

Questions to process:

What do I fear most? Where did this fear come from?

What do I think will happen if I face my fear?

After answering the questions above, I now understand:

Moving forward, I will:

What Are You Making it Mean?

Yesterday, I made a mistake. I overlooked an important task/deadline at work and boy did my inner critic try to eat me alive. That one mistake connected all of these harsh thoughts which surfaced criticisms such as: *"You're a failure", "you're not cut out for this," "you can't even get a simple task right," "you're going to ruin this experience for everyone and you should just stop while you're ahead."* These thoughts create feelings of defeat, regret, shame, fear and disappointment. Feeling these feelings made me want to hide, go home, distract myself and make an excuse. I had to get out of this mind drama. I needed to put my brain in its proper place and remind it who's boss, *me*!

I felt so out of control. My motivation had dwindled and those thoughts were getting the best of me. Then, it hit me. I can't do this alone. Let me reach out to someone I know who will help me get back on track. I called a coaching friend and word vomited all the mental drama I just experienced. She said, "Okay, let me get you off this ledge." She reminded me that I'm giving meaning to things that aren't true about my situation. She helped me see how I was trying to justify the negative thoughts. She showed me the ways I was unintentionally comparing and competing when I should have been seeking comprehension.

I was made aware of my attempt to be faultless instead of using this as a stepping stone to growth. Woah! She was *so right*. I needed that reminder. I had to examine my thoughts and find evidence for the accusations I made against myself. The verdict was out. I found no evidence to support my negative claims. I sat at my desk and envisioned myself doing everything at my highest ability. I asked myself, "*If you were your ultimate self in this role right now, what would you be thinking? What would you be feeling? How would you be acting? Who would be around you?*"

I reminded myself that I am human and my mistakes don't define me. I went for a walk, prayed, listened to a motivating song and got back to it. I created a new game plan and chose to operate at the highest level possible. I was grateful I invited someone in who could help me out of the mess I had created for no apparent reason.

I realized so many of us reach out for help when we have issues with our bodies, workout equipment or a project. We reach out when we can't create that hair style, make that recipe, or fix the toilet. In these instances, we reach out shamelessly. But, why is it so hard to reach out when we struggle with the thoughts and feelings that create undesirable experiences in our lives? What does it really mean when we refuse to ask for what we need, mentally and emotionally? Don't beat yourself up. Ask for what you need because we all need help along the journey.

Reflections:

After reading this passage, I realize:

Affirmation: *I am simply human and my mistakes don't define me.*

Questions to process:

How do I respond when I make big mistakes?

What do I need to do to accept the mistakes and move forward despite them?

After answering the questions above, I now understand:

Moving forward, I will:

Find Your People

It is said that you become like the people you spend the bulk of your time with. I intentionally surround myself with people who are: driven, filled with grace, courageous, believers, dreamers, and those who want the best for everyone, seek to understand, committed to learning for a lifetime, thought leaders, risk takers, and people who do hard things because they know that their results will far outweigh their sacrifice. I'm connected to people who desire critical feedback, offer honest opinions and understand the gift of reflection. They are uplifting, committed to growth, refuse to tell me what I want to hear and offer the truth that I need.

Today, I'm here to encourage you to find your people. Surround yourself with people who: see the best in you, are willing to walk with you in the worst of times, believe in your dreams and take an active role in helping you get there. Choose people who speak life into you. Be with people who inspire you to be better and who unapologetically welcome you to journey with them. Stay connected to people who take you to the next level and allow you to do the same for them. I have no words for these amazing humans that I get to call my tribe. I'm proud to know them and am all the better because of them. To my tribe: you are truly a gift to me! Thank you!

Take time out today to let your tribe know how much you love and appreciate them. The little things make all the difference.

Reflections:

After reading this passage, I realize:

Affirmation: *I am surrounded by people who inspire me and have my best interest at heart.*

Questions to process:

Who am I currently surrounded by and how are they helping me get to my next level?

Who, around me, is a source of inspiration? What about them inspires me?

After answering the questions above, I now understand:

Moving forward, I will:

Honoring Others By Honoring Yourself First

"People learn what they need to learn the way they choose to learn it, and there is nothing we can do about their choice."~Iyanla Vanzant, *One Day My Soul Just Opened Up*

I have lived much of my life acting as a savior, clearly seeing the destruction that lies ahead of others and taking on the responsibility to help them get to a "better place." The place I believed they should be and not necessarily the place they desired to be. I didn't want to live in the pain of watching them fall. I have found myself wanting for people more than they want for themselves, trying to convince them that they should want better too. Then, I came across Iyanla Vanzant's quote. "People learn what they need to learn the way they choose to learn it, and there is nothing we can do about their choice."

Everytime I tried to help someone and it didn't turn out the way I thought it should, I felt unappreciated, resentful, frustrated and misunderstood. This quote helped me understand how unknowingly prideful I was and how I have taken away others' power to choose when I made choices for them. I came to understand I was dishonoring them and getting in the way by thinking I knew what was best for them. What I was doing was dishonoring their choices. They never blatantly asked for the help I'd offered. The offer came from my judgment of their situation, based on my own fears.

I now understand that what I perceive as suffering and struggle, is the way people have chosen to learn their lesson in life. I must honor that! If people ask for help, then I get to choose how I would like to help; not out of obligation, but out of a way that brings me joy.

We have to honor our right to choose how we engage with others, while also honoring their choices and decisions for their lives. In order to truly honor others, we must first have a clear sense of what it means to honor ourselves. We must have a healthy relationship with boundaries. We need to operate from a place of respect for ourselves *and* others.

Also, just because you have a desire to help doesn't mean you are helping. We are living proof of our choices. If someone else's choices for their life are creating negative emotions inside of you, sit and think about what this is bringing up for you. Why are you focusing externally, instead of internally? What is the best way you can honor their choices without dishonoring yourself? I now know how to meet people where they are, not where I want them to be. I can walk alongside people, but I can't walk for them.

I am grateful for that revelation!

Reflections:

After reading this passage, I realize:

Affirmation: ***When I honor myself, I give myself greater ability to honor others.***

Questions to process:

Who am I currently trying to "save" or "help"? Why does "helping" them matter so much to me?

When was the last time I "helped" someone and it drained me? What boundaries should I have put in place?

After answering the questions above, I now understand:

Moving forward, I will:

I Am Worthy

Your self-worth is not determined by the opinions of others. Not being chosen does *not* mean you aren't good enough. A job, school, program or person does not define your destiny. Stop hoping that someone will see something in you that you don't see in yourself. Do the work so that you can clearly see how great you are. If you feel unworthy, what do you need to do to feel worthy? If you are unhappy with yourself, what will bring happiness into your life? If you don't like something about yourself, what are you willing to do to change it?

Truth is, you are enough just the way you are. Not because of what you do, have, or possess, simply because you are! It's your job to recognize, establish and confirm your worth. Some people may or may not recognize it, but don't allow others to decide your worthiness. Don't hope to be chosen. Instead, choose yourself. Become who you are seeking. Do things daily that make you feel proud of the life you are living!

Reflections:

After reading this passage, I realize:

Affirmation: *I am worthy simply because I am alive. My worth has already been recognized, established and confirmed by my mere existence.*

Questions to process:

Where does my sense of self-worth come from?

In what ways am I looking to others to validate my worth?

After answering the questions above, I now understand:

Moving forward, I will:

Believe in Your Vision

I've been called a dreamer, an optimist to a fault. People have shared that I expect too much of myself and my standards are too high. They ask me questions like, "Why do you have so many degrees?" "Why do you keep changing jobs?" "Why do you keep having kids back to back?" "Why do you keep moving from state to state?"

I've often internalized this feedback and questioned myself asking, *"Can I really do this? Is my bar too high? Am I not living in reality? Is my head too caught up in the clouds?"* Then, I'd begin to feel doubtful and fearful of my deepest desires. "What if I fail? Then they'll tell me "I told you so." What if.....? What if....? What if?

Then one day, I realized people are providing feedback based on their own reality, fears and limitations. Others may not be willing to put in the time and work to get the result they really want. But, I'm not like other people. I *will* get the results I choose because I *will put* in the work! I began to shift my "what if?" questions. What if I could lose eighty pounds in a year? What if I could create a life-changing business? What if I could send all of my kids to private school? What if I could rebuild top tier credit? My *what if's* have now been replaced by I *will*! You can't lose faith in yourself! What you feed your mind shapes your future. Your thoughts create your results. You must feed your mind with success and belief.

My thoughts, beliefs, and actions are strong. No matter what people say, I believe I can obtain all that I set out to accomplish because I know that I am powerful beyond measure. Don't let others' visions or beliefs stop you. Your dreams are not too big. Keep dreaming. Your goals are not unrealistic. Keep crushing them. Who you are is not too much. Keep being *you*! You deserve to experience your wildest dreams. So get to work and don't give up. Your best self and greatest life are waiting to greet you!

Reflections:

After reading this passage, I realize:

Affirmation: *My greatest self and greatest life await me. I will obtain all that I set out to accomplish.*

Questions to process:

What feedback have others given me that has made me feel doubtful?

Why does this feedback bother me?

After answering the questions above, I now understand:

Moving forward, I will:

Appearance Isn't Everything

Many people have told me that when they first met me, they thought, "She has it made. She is stuck up. She is a know-it-all." Truthfully, people judge from their level of knowledge. My faith, vision and implemented goals are what helped me to build a life I feel proud of. Yes, I have a family, career and beautiful community. But all of these things take work to maintain. The reality isn't always pretty, but it's *always worth* it.

People will judge the result because they're not looking when you are working. They don't see the vision or process. They simply analyze and comment about the results. Confidence is often mistaken for arrogance. Yes, I am assertive, outspoken and ambitious. But, I do not elevate my stature by diminishing others, deflect my flaws or believe I'm superior. I genuinely love connecting with people and learning their stories. I love teaching people to live in possibility and inspiration. I enjoy helping people operate from a place of passion, empathy, and drive. I believe in life-long learning and loving people fiercely!

People will always be on the outside looking in, filled with questions, opinions and concerns. Regardless of their judgment, always remember that misunderstandings happen. It is not your job to defend who you are. Simply *be yourself*. How you see yourself is more important than how others see you. The only thing that matters is how you feel about yourself. If you are unhappy with your habits, attitude, or experience, change it! You are powerful and deserve to experience the best that life can offer.

Reflections:

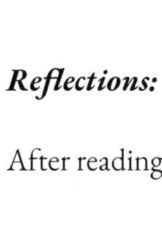

After reading this passage, I realize:

Affirmation: *I am important, I matter and I will experience the best that life has to offer.*

Questions to process:

What feedback have I received about other peoples' impressions of me?

What do I think about this feedback?

After answering the questions above, I now understand:

Moving forward, I will:

About the Author:

Cynque Milagro is an author, liberation coach, consultant, poet and speaker. Her passion is to create, and be a part of, experiences that restore lives, renew minds and change hearts. She is fueled by helping others discover their talents and lead purposeful lives. She helps others realize the impact that mindset and belief have on the human ability to live in an authentically purposeful way. She also enjoys helping people build lives they are proud of, with special attention to growth mindset, self-awareness and goal setting.

@coachcynque

www.coachcynque.com

Made in the USA
Columbia, SC
05 September 2022